Revolutionary WOMEN

From Colonists to Suffragists

COMPILED BY THE
PETER PAUPER PRESS EDITORS

Peter Pauper Press, Inc.
WHITE PLAINS, NEW YORK

PETER PAUPER PRESS
Fine Books and Gifts Since 1928

OUR COMPANY

In 1928, at the age of twenty-two, Peter Beilenson bgan printing books on a small press in the basement of his parents' home in Larchmont, New York. Peter—and later, his wife, Edna—sought to create fine books that sold at "prices even a pauper could afford."

Today, still family owned and operated, Peter Pauper Press continues to honor our founders' legacy—and our customers' expectations—of beauty, quality, and value.

To Angela: Even the littlest person
can make the biggest difference.

Images used under license from Shutterstock.com
and sourced from Wikimedia Commons.
Images of Rebecca Lukens and Julia Morgan: Robert J. Schwalb.
Image of Ellen Browning Scripps courtesy
University of California, San Diego.

Designed by Heather Zschock

Visit us at www.peterpauper.com

To:

From:

Revolutionary WOMEN

────── ⚬⚬⚬ ──────

From Colonists to Suffragists

Contents

Introduction

The proving ground on which we stand as women is comprised of milestones achieved by our visionary sisters of the past. From all walks of life and with an amazing range of accomplishments, female revolutionaries triumphed against the odds in opening doors for those who followed.

From the woman who printed the first edition of the Declaration of Independence listing the names of all the signers, to the interpreter and peacemaker who was essential to the discovery of the West, to the conductor of the Underground Railroad, to the first woman to run for President in 1872, to "possibly the best sharpshooter

had a son, Thomas. The family then visited England, where she was presented to the royal family. Sadly, Pocahontas, now Rebecca Rolfe, became ill, died en route back home, and was buried in Gravesend, England. This remarkable young woman's life was brief, just 21 or 22 years, but her legend as a peacemaker and ambassador lives on more than 400 years later.

Mercy Otis Warren

1728–1814

"Democratic principles are the result of equality of condition."

America's first female playwright, **Mercy Otis Warren** has been called the "muse" and "secret pen" of the American Revolution. Born on Cape Cod, she was a sister to impassioned patriot James Otis. She married James Warren, who became one of George Washington's generals; they had five children. Warren was acquainted with many of the Revolution's early leaders, including John and Abigail Adams, George and Martha Washington, and Thomas Jefferson. A prolific writer, she produced—often using pseudonyms— poems, essays, pamphlets, and plays, much of her work deriding the British.

Her 1772 play, *The Adulateur,* featured
an antagonist character based on
Thomas Hutchinson, the royal governor
of Massachusetts. She also wrote one of
the first histories of the Revolutionary
War: *History of the Rise, Progress, and
Termination of the American Revolution,*
in three volumes. It was published
in 1805.

Mary Katharine Goddard

1738–1816

"Baltimore, in Maryland:
Printed by Mary Katharine Goddard."

Notice at the bottom of the first printed edition
of the Declaration of Independence to include
the names of the signers.

Patriot **Mary Katharine Goddard** was
the first woman in America to hold a
federal office—that of Postmaster of
Baltimore. Appointed by Benjamin
Franklin, she held the office for
14 years. Goddard was also one of
America's first female newspaper
publishers, chronicling Revolutionary
battles in the *Maryland Journal* for a
news-hungry public. She was a book-
seller and ran a print shop; her brother
William said she was "an expert and

correct compositor of types." In 1777, the Continental Congress, meeting in Baltimore at the time, commissioned Goddard to print the first edition of the Declaration of Independence to include the signers' names. Twelve years later, to her frustration, Goddard was relieved of her position as Postmaster for political reasons, but not before 200 Baltimore businessmen vigorously protested. Goddard continued to operate her bookstore until her early seventies.

Nancy Ward, or Nanye'hi

1738–1822 or 1824

"Princess and Prophetess of the Cherokee Nation, the Pocahontas of Tennessee, the constant Friend of the American Pioneer."

Inscription on a plaque at Nancy Ward's grave near Benton, Tennessee.

Cherokee **Nancy Ward**, or **Nanye'hi**, "One who is with the Spirit People," was a powerful tribeswoman in the mid- to late-1700s, and said to be the last Cherokee Agi-ga-u-e, or "Beloved Woman." Born in Tennessee, Ward was the daughter of a Cherokee woman named Tame Doe and an Irishman, Francis Ward. As a Beloved Woman, Ward sat in on council meetings with male and female leaders and the colonists. Ward advocated co-existence

with white settlers and white military forces during the French and Indian and Revolutionary Wars. She assisted in negotiating a treaty between the Cherokee and the colonists, enabling American forces to defeat the British in 1781, signaling the beginning of the end of the Revolution. She advocated that her people keep their lands and take up farming; she is said to be the first Cherokee cattle owner.

Phillis Wheatley

Circa 1753–1784

"In every human Beast, God has implanted a Principle, which we call Love of Freedom; it is impatient of Oppression, and pants for Deliverance."

Phillis Wheatley was the first African American to publish a book. Kidnapped at age seven from West Africa and taken to Boston on a slave ship, she was purchased by John Wheatley, a tailor, as a servant for his wife, Susanna. The Wheatleys named her Phillis and taught her to read and write, not only in English, but in Latin and Greek. Phillis began to write poetry about religion and morality, and about the people, issues, and events of her time. She wrote her first published

say "Captain Molly" even took the place of her husband, William Hays, in the gun crew after he either collapsed or was wounded. Others say Washington himself commended Mary for her efforts. According to records, William Hays did enlist in the Army in 1776; he passed away in 1789. Mary Hays applied for a soldier's widow's pension and was awarded an annual grant of 40 dollars "for services she rendered."

Dolley Madison

1768–1849

"It is one of my sources of happiness never to desire a knowledge of other people's business."

An Early American "hostess with the mostest," **Dolley Payne Todd Madison**, wife of two-term President James Madison, set a White House standard for first ladies to come. Born in North Carolina, Dolley married John Todd at the age of 22. They had two sons, but a 1793 yellow fever epidemic killed her husband and younger son, leaving her a widow and single parent at age 25. Aaron Burr introduced her to James Madison, 17 years her senior. Madison proposed and she accepted. Smart and vivacious, Dolley was popular in Washington, D.C.,

circles; she even served in the capacity of
first lady for President Thomas Jefferson,
a widower. Dolley is especially famous for
saving White House valuables, including
the iconic Lansdowne portrait of George
Washington by Gilbert Stuart, during the
War of 1812, when the British set fire
to Washington. She returned to the city
and to her duty mere days later, hosting
gatherings to buoy the spirits of capital
inhabitants.

Sacajawea

Circa 1788–1812

"Everything I do is for my people."

The daughter of a Shoshone chief, **Sacajawea**, born in Idaho, was kidnapped by Hidatsa warriors and sold to a French-Canadian fur trader named Toussaint Charbonneau at about age 13. The trapper married her, then volunteered both himself and Sacajawea as guides for Meriwether Lewis's and William Clark's expedition west in 1804, even though his young wife would need to carry their weeks-old infant son, Jean-Baptiste, on her back. Lewis and Clark valued Sacajawea's presence; they knew tribes they met along the way would understand that they were not warmongers, because a woman accompanied them. And Sacajawea could help

them when they reached Shoshone
territory. She did; her brother had become
a tribal leader, and provided fresh horses
for the expedition. Sacajawea was also an
interpreter, peacemaker, and forager of
food. She saved valuable equipment when
a canoe capsized. The expedition reached
the Pacific Ocean in November 1805;
Sacajawea led them back again. In 1812,
Sacajawea bore a daughter, Lisette, but
died soon after the birth. William Clark
adopted both her children in 1813.

Emma Willard

1787–1870

"Genuine learning has ever been said to give polish to man; why then should it not bestow added charm on women?"

Emma Willard, née Emma Hart, one of 17 children, demonstrated a hunger for learning at an early age. Enrolled in her first school at 15, she became a teacher there just two years later. Ten years later, she started a school in the home she shared with her husband, John Willard, a physician. Emma showed that women could learn the same subjects as men, and wrote "An Address to the Public" on this topic in 1819. Her views were supported by Thomas Jefferson and John Adams, among others, and New York State governor DeWitt Clinton invited her to

start a school. Emma started the Troy,
New York, Female Seminary in 1821,
the first school in the United States
to teach women science, philosophy,
mathematics, and more. It became a
prestigious institution and is known
today as the Emma Willard School,
or simply "Emma." Alumni include
activist Elizabeth Cady Stanton, actor
Jane Fonda, and Senator Kirsten
Gillibrand.

Rebecca Lukens

1794–1854

*"I had built a very superior mill,
though a plain one, and our character
for making boiler iron stood first in the
market, hence we had as much business as
we could do. . . . There was difficulty and
danger on every side. Now I look back
and wonder at my daring."*

Rebecca Lukens, née Rebecca Webb
Pennock, was the "First Lady of Iron
and Steel," according to *Fortune*
magazine. In 1793, on Pennsylvania's
Brandywine River, her father, Isaac
Pennock, founded the Federal Slitting
Mill, which made metal strips used in
barrel- and wheel-making. Rebecca,
oldest of seven children, took an inter-
est in the business; about 20 years after
the mill's founding, her new husband,

Dr. Charles Lukens, became a
partner. Later, he leased Isaac's new
Brandywine Iron Works. Their
businesses expanded with the advent
of steam power, producing boilerplates
for shipbuilding and track for railroads.
After her father's death in 1824, and
Charles's death in 1825, Rebecca took
over. She focused on manufacturing
quality products, treating employees
well, and refusing to cater to customers
who made weapons of war.

Sojourner Truth

Circa 1797–1883

"Life is a hard battle anyway. If we laugh and sing a little as we fight the good fight of freedom, it makes it all go easier. I will not allow my life's light to be determined by the darkness around me."

Sojourner Truth was born in New York State as a slave named **Isabella Baumfree** and sold away from her parents when she was nine years old. She married another slave and had five children, all but one of whom were sold. When she was legally able to leave her owner, he refused; Isabella escaped with her daughter in 1826. She went to court in 1828 to get her son Peter back; he had been sold to a man in Alabama, and she became the first black woman to win such a case. In 1843, Isabella had a

vision instructing her to become a preacher. She took the name "Sojourner," meaning "Traveler," and said when she asked God for a last name, "The Lord gave me Truth, because I was to declare the truth to the people." She became a powerful speaker, abolitionist, and women's rights advocate. Her extemporaneous speech, "Ain't I a Woman?" delivered at an 1851 woman's convention in Ohio, is her best known. Sojourner Truth continued preaching well into her eighties.

Harriet Beecher Stowe

1811–1896

"Never give up, for that is just the place and time that the tide will turn."

Born **Harriet Elisabeth Beecher** in Litchfield, Connecticut, the future author and abolitionist grew up in a prominent and well-educated family. She and her sister, Catharine, moved with their father to Cincinnati, Ohio, in 1832, where she met and married clergyman and professor Calvin Ellis Stowe. In Ohio, Harriet encountered slaves who had escaped across the Ohio River and visited the South herself. After moving to Maine with her husband when he took a position at Bowdoin College, Harriet began to

write, in serial form, what would eventually become *Uncle Tom's Cabin; or Life Among the Lowly*, which was published as a book in 1852. The book revealed the cruelties and conditions of slavery in narrative form. Even though Stowe was not an established writer, the book became a phenomenon, selling an incredible 300,000 copies in its first year alone, and is cited as one of the causes of the Civil War.

Harriet Jacobs

1813–1897

"The beautiful spring came; and when Nature resumes her loveliness, the human soul is apt to revive also."

Harriet Ann Jacobs was born into slavery in North Carolina, but according to her writings, lived in a protected environment until she was six, when she was orphaned and went to live with her mother's mistress. Upon her death, she became the property of a man named James Norcom, who sexually abused her. Harriet hid in a crawl space for seven years to escape Norcom's advances, and took as a lover a young white lawyer, Samuel Tredwell Sawyer. The couple had two children, who were purchased by Sawyer and sent north. Jacobs escaped in 1842 and

she eventually moved to Rochester,
New York, where she worked in a
reading room above the offices of
Frederick Douglass's publication,
The North Star. She wrote and self-
published her autobiography, *Incidents
in the Life of a Slave Girl* in 1861. Her
story was lost during the ensuing years,
but brought to light once more during
the 1960s. At first thought to be a
fictional narrative, it was authenticated
by scholars in 1981.

Elizabeth Cady Stanton

1815–1902

"The best protection any woman can have . . . is courage."

Elizabeth Cady, born in Johnstown, New York, attended Emma Willard's famed Female Seminary in Troy, New York. She fell in love and married abolitionist Henry B. Stanton in 1840; they had seven children and eventually moved to Seneca Falls. In 1848, with the help of activist Lucretia Mott, Elizabeth organized the First Women's Rights Convention. Here she presented a "Declaration of Sentiments," based on the Declaration of Independence, proclaiming the equality of the sexes. Elizabeth went on to further efforts for women's rights and suffrage, the

abolition of slavery, divorce law liberalization, and the right of "self-sovereignty," in which women take deliberate measures to avoid pregnancy. Her growing liberal views resulted in her controversial contact with "free-lover" Victoria Woodhull and clash with the conservative Woman's Christian Temperance Union, but Cady Stanton continued fighting for women's rights until her death in 1902.

Lucy Stone

1818–1893

"Now all we need is to continue to speak the truth fearlessly, and we shall add to our number those who will turn the scale to the side of equal and full justice in all things."

Born in West Brookfield, Massachusetts, **Lucy Stone** was the first American woman to keep her maiden name after marriage. A determined child, Lucy insisted on studying Hebrew and Greek so she could learn if certain biblical passages that were said to give men control over women were correctly translated. She graduated from Oberlin College in 1847, and began lecturing for the Massachusetts Anti-Slavery Society and for women's rights. She also organized several

women's rights conventions. She
married abolitionist Henry Blackwell
in 1855. She kept her maiden name
in protest of the inequality of married
women, and became known as Mrs.
Stone. In 1869, with Julia Ward Howe,
she organized the American Woman
Suffrage Association. Stone founded the
Woman's Journal, a weekly periodical,
which published differing views on
women's rights.

Julia Ward Howe

1819–1910

"The strokes of the pen need deliberation as much as the sword needs swiftness."

Born in New York City, **Julia Ward** was an abolitionist, women's rights activist, and a poet. She married Samuel Howe, who became director of the Perkins Institute for the Blind in Boston. Though her husband opposed Julia's having a public life, she began writing poems and plays. Her "Battle Hymn of the Republic," inspired by an 1861 visit to Washington, D.C., in which she met Abraham Lincoln, was written to the tune of "John Brown's Body." It was published in *The Atlantic Monthly* in 1862, and became an unofficial song of the Union Army. Julia went on to help found the New England Woman

Suffrage Association, was active in a number of other women's groups, and was the first woman elected to the American Academy of Arts and Letters in 1908.

Harriet Tubman

1820–1913

"Always remember, you have within you the strength, the patience, and the passion to reach for the stars to change the world."

Harriet Tubman was born a slave named **Araminta Ross** in Maryland. She suffered a severe head injury as a teenager, which gave her hallucinations and sleeping spells throughout her life. She married John Tubman in 1844. She escaped in 1849 and changed her first name to Harriet, after her mother. She became the most famous "conductor" of the Underground Railroad, guiding more than 300 slaves to freedom. During the Civil War, Harriet worked as a nurse, cook, spy, and scout. She supported herself and those she helped with donations and with money she

raised from the proceeds of her vegetable garden. She eventually raised enough money to open schools for African Americans and began speaking about women's rights. She also dreamed of founding a home for the elderly; in 1908 her Harriet Tubman Home for the Aged opened in Auburn, New York. Harriet lived there herself until her death in 1913.

Emily Dickinson

1828–1886

"If I read a book and it makes my whole body so cold no fire can ever warm me, I know that is poetry."

Born in Amherst, Massachusetts, the second of three children, **Emily Elizabeth Dickinson** was the granddaughter of one of the founders of Amherst College. As a girl, she excelled in Latin, composition, and science, especially botany; she is said to have created an extensive herbarium of pressed plants. Dickinson began composing verse in her teenage years. In her late twenties, she copied her poems onto stationery sheets and made them into small books. She assembled about 40 of these books, which contained hundreds of poems.

Famously reclusive, and famously prolific, Dickinson, (along with Walt Whitman), is considered one of the two leading poets of the 19th century. She wrote nearly 1,800 poems, but only ten were published during her lifetime (and were likely edited by the publications' editors). Her poems are considered bold, original, and free of the poetic rules of the time.

Harriet Goodhue Hosmer

1830–1908

*"Even if so inclined, an artist
has no business to marry. For a man,
it may be well enough, but for a woman,
on whom matrimonial duties and cares
weigh more heavily, it is a moral wrong,
for she must either neglect her family,
or her profession."*

The first professional female sculptor,
Harriet Goodhue Hosmer, a Neoclas-
sicist, was a self-taught artist who ini-
tially worked in a home studio, taking
private lessons in anatomy. At the age
of 22, Harriet went to Rome to study
with prominent British sculptor John
Gibson, and flourished in the city's
expatriate community, with Robert and
Elizabeth Barrett Browning among her

friends and acquaintances. She completed her first professional work four years later, and a steady stream of commissions ensued. Harriet's 1855 sculpture of *Puck*, the character from Shakespeare's *Midsummer Night's Dream*, sold a number of copies; one was purchased by Albert Edward, Prince of Wales.

Mary Harris "Mother" Jones

1830–1930

*"I'm not a humanitarian.
I'm a hell-raiser."*

Born in County Cork, Ireland, **Mary Harris Jones** was no stranger to misfortune, losing her family to yellow fever and her home and dress shop to the Great Chicago Fire. She'd worked as a teacher and dressmaker, but left those professions behind to become a labor activist. She began to travel and speak, appearing at strike sites, addressing railroad workers and miners. By 1877, she had acquired her nickname of "Mother," and by 1902, she acquired another: "The most dangerous woman in America." She campaigned for United Mine Workers, founded the

Social Democratic Party, and helped found the Industrial Workers of the World. In 1903, she organized a children's march from Philadelphia to New York to reform child labor laws. In 1912, at age 82, she was arrested in a West Virginia strike. Upon her release, she returned to her work. She died in 1930. *Mother Jones* magazine, known for its investigative journalism, is named after her.

Victoria Woodhull

1838–1927

"While others prayed for the good time coming, I worked for it."

Maverick reformer **Victoria Woodhull**, née Victoria Clafin, was the first woman nominated for the American presidency in 1872 at the age of 34. (She would not have been able to vote for herself, however, as women did not possess the right to vote until 1920.) Born in Homer, Ohio, Victoria and her sister, Tennessee "Tennie" Clafin, were part of a traveling family act, peddling home remedies and psychic readings. Victoria was married twice by the time she was 30, when she and Tennie went to New York City, met magnate Cornelius Vanderbilt, and, with his assistance, set up the first woman-owned

Wall Street stockbrokerage. Its success allowed them to start a weekly women's rights magazine which featured discussions of free love and other scandalous topics. Victoria's ongoing efforts on behalf of woman's suffrage were so persuasive, she spoke on the topic in 1871 before the Judiciary Committee of the U.S. House of Representatives.

Annie Oakley

1860–1926

"Aim for the high mark and you will hit it. No, not the first time, not the second time and maybe not the third. But keep on aiming and keep on shooting, for only practice will make you perfect. Finally, you'll hit the bull's-eye of success."

From the age of eight, when she shot her first squirrel near her home in rural Ohio, **Annie Oakley**, born Phoebe Ann Mosey (or Moses) exhibited an uncanny ability to use firearms. By the time she was 15, according to legend, she had shot and sold—to restaurants, hotels, and food provisioners—enough game to pay off the family farm. That same year, Annie bested 28-year-old Vaudeville marksman Frank E. Butler in a shooting contest; they soon

married and stayed together for more than 50 years. The pair joined Buffalo Bill Cody's Wild West Show in 1885, and "Little Sure Shot" (a nickname given to her by Lakota chief Sitting Bull) became one of the first international female stars, performing before the likes of England's Queen Victoria and German Crown Prince Wilhelm. She continued to set marksmanship records well into her sixties.

Annie Jump Cannon

1863–1941

*"In these days of great trouble
and unrest, it is good to have something
outside our own planet, something
fine and distant . . . . Let people look
to the stars for comfort."*

Annie Jump Cannon developed her
love of stargazing as a child, when she
looked up into the night sky from
the roof of her Delaware home. Years
later, she was a star physics student at
Wellesley College in Massachusetts,
though the cold winter nights caused
ongoing ear infections that later led to
Annie's becoming deaf. After gradu-
ating in 1884, and after an unhappy
ten-year hiatus back home, she enrolled
at Radcliffe, Harvard's women's college,

to study astronomy. Her initiative and abilities led Harvard Observatory director Edward C. Pickering to select her for an intensive project: that of cataloging all the stars up to the ninth magnitude (16 times fainter than the human eye can see). Annie went on to identify and classify more than 5,000 stars a month; 350,000 stars total, more than any other astronomer.

Nellie Bly

1864–1922

*"Energy rightly applied and directed
will accomplish anything."*

Daring journalist **Nellie Bly** is perhaps
best known for posing as a mental
patient to expose conditions in the
Blackwell Island (now Roosevelt Island)
asylum in New York City in 1887.
Born Elizabeth Cochran in Cochran's
Mills, Pennsylvania, she got her start
in journalism at 18, after submitting
a spirited rebuttal to a sexist editorial
piece in the *Pittsburgh Dispatch*. The
paper's editor hired her and she began
to write stories under the pseudonym
"Nellie Bly" (after the 1850 Stephen
Foster song "Nelly Bly"). She moved
to New York two years later and began
working for the *New York World*. She

experienced life as a patient for ten days on Blackwell Island; her subsequent exposé made her famous. She also set a real-world record (72 days, 6 hours, 11 minutes, 14 seconds) circumnavigating the world—by ship, burro, rickshaw, sampan, and more—to beat the fictional record of the Jules Verne character, Phileas Fogg, of *Around the World in Eighty Days*.

Edmonia Lewis

or *Suhkuhegarequa*
(Chippewa for "Fire-making woman" or "Wildfire")

Circa 1844–1907

"Ohnishe shin." ("It is good.")

The daughter of an African American father and Native American mother, **Mary Edmonia Lewis** became a professional sculptor who achieved international fame. Born in upstate New York, Lewis attended Oberlin College in Ohio. She became known for her bust of Colonel Robert Gould Shaw, the Union hero from Boston who led black troops in the Civil War. The success of this piece enabled Lewis to move to Rome, Italy, where she began working in marble among her contemporaries, such as Harriet Hosmer. Lewis's sculptures depicted

Neoclassical, biblical, and abolitionist themes, and Lewis also incorporated both Native American and African American themes into her art. Perhaps her most famous piece was *The Death of Cleopatra*, which was exhibited at the 1876 Philadelphia Centennial Exposition. It is now owned by the Smithsonian American Art Museum. Lewis died in London in 1907.

Julia Morgan

1872-1957

"My buildings will be my legacy. They will speak for me long after I am gone."

The first licensed female architect in California, **Julia Morgan** designed newspaper magnate William Randolph Hearst's famous San Simeon castle, "Enchanted Hills." As a girl, Julia, born in San Francisco, was inspired by a cousin's architect husband. She was among the first women to enroll in Berkeley's College of Engineering, where she met and was influenced by Bernard Maybeck, an Arts and Craft Movement architect. Maybeck encouraged Julia to apply to the famous École des Beaux-Arts in Paris. Julia moved to France, where, after taking the institution's entrance exam three

times, she became the first woman to attend the school. Upon graduation, she returned to San Francisco, opening her own practice after a few years. Julia designed hotels, homes, and churches, but is best known for Hearst's complex, a 20-year project requiring her to travel hundreds of miles by train and car three times a month, while working on other commissions. She retired in 1951, having completed more than 700 projects.

*Every great
dream begins with
a dreamer.*

–HARRIET TUBMAN